Lord, Teach Us to Pray

(Luke 11:1)

by

Teri Hines

Lord, Teach Us to Pray

Contents

Dedication

Dedicated to the memory of

my beloved

Father and Mother

Inspired by the Holy Spirit for the

Glory of God

Through the Lord Jesus Christ

PREFACE

Praise Jesus from the pen of Teri Hines, who has written another engaging book with an immense message of the reasons and necessity of *Lord, Teach Us to Pray*. Hopefully, the reader will be motivated to strive and achieve a consistent and persistent prayer life that demonstrates sincere prayer of faith acceptable and pleasing to God our Savior.

Within these pages, you the reader will find encouragements that will inspire, I believe, their urgency to make a priority to develop and maintain a spontaneous urge to pray as St. Luke 18:1 demands, "Pray Without Ceasing." The writer is an anointed teacher, who has a magnificent prayer life. Therefore, she is truly concerned about the body of Christ—understanding and discovering the secret of a committed prayer life with our Father who art in heaven.

Because of the noteworthy power of prayer in a believer's life, it will serve as a guiding light in drawing all prayer warriors closer to God our Father. I trust the readers will meditate on the importance of praying and their hearts will cry unto the "Father thank you for helping me to obtain a beneficial life of prayer".

Teri suggests the secret on how to stay on a spiritual high while growing in the grace and knowledge of Jesus Christ. She advocates that prayer will stimulate the Body of Christ to continue with an unshakable relationship with God Almighty. According to Jude (Verse 20), here is what required, "But you, beloved, building up yourselves on your most holy faith, praying in the Holy Ghost." Be intentional and discover the potential secret, in the power of prayer.

Delores Clyburn, Your Dear Sister in Christ

THANK YOU

Father, Thank You that our prayers are a sweet incense to Your nostril.

Revelation 8:4

John 3:16-17

"For God so loved the world that He gave His only begotten Son, that whoever believes in Him should not perish but have everlasting life. For God did not send His Son into the world to condemn the world, but that the world through Him might be saved."

According to the Strong's Concordance. the Greek word for loved is 'agapao'.

The Greek Word Study defined 'agapao' as to love unconditionally and sacrificially as God Himself loves sinful men the way He loves the Son and noted that 'agapao' is a verb and by its verbal nature calls for action. This quality of love is not an emotion but is an action initiated by a volitional choice

The Merriam-Webster Dictionary defined volitional as the act or the power of making a choice or decision.

In other words, this God of the universe, the Creator of heaven and earth by His own will gave His only begotten Son, so that He may have other sons. It is all because of love and through love.

We are to know that we are loved by God.

Purpose

The purpose of writing this book is to bring the reader to his/hers knees in the heart of acknowledging God in His Magnificence, realizing His awesome glory. This book is designed to have the hearts of the reader fused with God's heart. Uniting with God in prayer will draw us closer to Him.

Hopefully, the reader will sense and know the love of God and that there is no greater love.

The Father's Desire

I Chronicles 29:10-13

"Blessed are You, Lord God of Israel, Our Father, forever and ever. Yours, O Lord, is the greatness, the power and the glory, the victory, and the majesty; For all that is in heaven and in earth is Yours; Yours is the kingdom, O Lord, And You are exalted as head over all. Both riches and honor come from You, and You reign over all. In Your hand is power and might; In Your hand it is to make great and to give strength to all. Now therefore, our God, we thank You and praise Your glorious name."

This Glorious God has chosen to love us, and desires that we may have a relationship with Him that His abode may be with us and in us. This love from the Father is lifegiving, everlasting, bountiful, awesome, and self-less. God's love was manifested throughout all the earth that He gave His only begotten Son that whoever believes in Him should not perish but will have everlasting life[1].

May the reason we pray is to commune and develop a relationship with the Father, because He first loved us and in return that we may love Him. Let our relationship in prayer be one of love. This special and private place of communion in prayer is where we learn the characteristics of the Father, to hear His voice, and to learn His heart.

Let our prayer life be a language of love so that His will may be done on this earth.

---

[1] John 3:16

Jewels of thought

What are the possibilities of Faith? The possibilities are endless.

What is the strength of Joy? It is life-giving.

What is this magnificence of Grace? It is the sweetness of the Holy Spirit.

Love has endurable power.

Praying Time

What is prayer?

Revelations 5:8

"Now when He had taken the scroll, the four living creatures and the twenty-four elders fell down before the lamb, each having a harp, and golden bowls full of incense, which are the prayers of the saints."

Definitions of prayer that are according to the Strong's Exhaustive Concordance of the Bible.

Old Testament Definitions:
'Athar' – to burn incense in worship; intercede, intreat
'Chaan' – to beseech (ask urgently and fervently to do something)
'Chalah' – to entreat
'Palal' – to judge (officially or mentally) by extension to intercede, intreat, supplication
'Shaal' 'Shael' – to request
'Siyach' – to converse
'Ts^{E}la' – to bow

New Testament Definitions:
'Deomai' – to beg, i.e., petition, make a request
'Erotao' – to request
'Euchomai' – petition to God
'Parakaleo' – to call near, to invite
'Proseuche' – to worship
'Proseuchomai' – to supplicate

Holman Bible Dictionary defined prayer as the dialogue between God and people, especially His covenant partners.

Wikipedia defined prayer as in the Hebrew Bible as an evolving means of interacting with God, most frequently through a spontaneous, individual, unorganized form of petitioning and/or thanking. The act of praying is a method of changing a situation for the better.

Wycliffe Dictionary defined prayer as "calling upon the name of the Lord."

Zondervan Bible Dictionary defined prayer as the spiritual response (spoken and unspoken) to God, who is known not merely to exist but to have revealed Himself and to have invited His creatures into communion with Himself.

My definition of prayer is having an intimate, purposeful, and intentional interaction by conversating with God—the lower (us) manifesting our dependency upon the higher (God) through Jesus Christ by the Holy Spirit. Prayer defines our relationship with God and is our response to the command of our Lord, *"that men always ought to pray."*[2] The New Compact Bible Dictionary states that prayer is a Biblical force and I concur.

Prayer is a manner of honoring God; this puts us in a position of humility submitting oneself to a higher authority.

Prayer is an act of worship acknowledging His Sovereignty, authority, all-knowing, all-powerful, all-present, all-loving. The One who is the author of life. God is the creator of heaven and earth that has life in the palm of His hand. God our Father is the Alpha and Omega.

It is a delight and privilege to be able to address or draw near to God. It is God's good pleasure to have a relationship with His beloved children. Prayer offers to us the privilege and opportunity of inviting God into our lives so that His will may be done.

Yes, the Lord of lords has given us an invitation to commune with Him. Written in Isaiah 1:18, *"Come now, and let us reason together."* To commune with God is to have an intimate relationship with Him.

Prayer is taking the time to dialogue with God. The Merriam-Webster Dictionary defined dialogue as a conversation between two or more parties and defined conversation as an informal talking together. Hopefully, we will realize with whom we are having this

---

[2] Luke 18:1

dialogue—it is with the God of gods, Creator of heaven and earth, the King of Glory—and the charge is to believe that we will receive a response from this personable God.

Prayer is to intreat God. Free Dictionary defined intreat as 1. To ask (a person) earnestly; beseech; implore; beg. 2. To ask earnestly for something.

Genesis 4:26 (qara) recorded the first occurrence when men called on the name of the Lord. "And as for Seth, to him also a son was born; and he named him Enosh. Then men began to call on the name of the Lord."

Recorded in *Genesis 12:8, "And he (Abram) moved from there to the mountain east of Bethel, and he pitched his tent with Bethel on the west and Ai on the east; there he built an altar to the Lord and called on the name of the Lord."*

This Old Testament Hebrew word for call is 'qara'; the Strong's Concordance defined call as to cry out, proclaim, to address by name, proclaim pronounce, publish.

The Greek word for 'call' is 'epikaleomai' defined in the Strong's Concordance as to invoke for aid, worship, testimony, decisions, etc.

Acts 2:21, "And it shall come to pass that whoever calls on the name of the Lord shall be saved."

Romans 10:13-14, "For whoever calls on the name of the Lord shall be saved. How then shall they call on Him in whom they have not believed? And how shall they believe in Him of whom they have not heard? And how shall they hear without a preacher?"

Whether we call, intreat, or pray, this depicts our dependency on the Lord. *"It is in Him we live, move, and have our being."*[3]

Prayer is a mindful and heartfelt conversation with God our Father. When we are conversing with the Lord, hopefully, we will realize

---

[3] Acts 17:28

that our conversations are divine dialogues with the Creator of heaven and earth. Prayer is not to be mundane (lacking interest or excitement; dull), but to be purposeful, exciting, and intentional. What do you want to discuss with the Lord?

Prayers are to be intentional and purposeful with the understanding to whom we are connecting—having a deliberate mindset of talking with God, in other words having your focus on God.

We often hear people say that prayer is communing with God. Do we understand that communing with God is to share one's intimate thoughts or feelings? Are we intentional or deliberate with Him?

It is so impressive to have the God of gods, the Creator of heaven and earth, the designer of all the universe and the cosmos to want to spend time with us—to call on His name—not in the sense of being a dictator, but as a loving Father.

In the Bible, the Prophet of Old, said when he considered the handiwork of God, he then asked the question, *"What is man, that thou art mindful of him?"*[4] This should put us in an amazement that we are fellowshipping with the King of Glory. What high profile person can you fellowship with while having coffee or tea able to express your most heartfelt intimate feelings? Knowing that your feelings will be confidential and safe. He wants to commune with you while you are living everyday life.

Optimistically, we will know and understand that the time we spend with God our Father is a spiritual connection which causes a divine relationship. Also, to have the understanding that prayer is a response to God's love for us and that we may reciprocate our love to Him by cultivating an unbreakable relationship having a solid foundation.

In the past, while praying, I would find myself being absent minded. I realized that I was just saying words that did not involve my heart or mind. Scriptures and words were just flowing from my mouth without any bearing of life and I had to shake myself to return to

---

[4] Psalm 8:4 (KJV)

the reality of my conversation with God. When my heart and mind were void of meaningful conversation, then the question presented itself: Was this really praying or was it just talking to be talking? *'God, please help me.'* Hopefully, our prayers are not empty routine words with our Father of Heaven. He is the reason for our being and lifeless prayers does not add any value.

Prayers, prayers, prayers; we often hear that we are to pray. There are Bible studies on prayer, prayer groups, prayer meetings, this list can go on and on.

According to LifeCoach4God.life, there are 650 prayers recorded in the Bible.

There are numerous examples in the Bible of renowned people praying to God. We can take account of Abraham, Moses, Daniel, Peter, Paul, etc. Throughout the Bible there are demonstrations of people praying to God, but our greatest example of a person of prayer is our Lord Jesus Christ.

In the New Testament section of the Bible, the Lord Jesus said in *John 5:19, "The Son can do nothing of Himself, but what He sees the Father do; for whatever He does, the Son also does in like manner."* How can this be? This can take place through fellowship with God our Father by remaining in prayer, reading, and studying the Scriptures. The Lord Jesus was in constant communication with His Father. What an example to His followers.

Whether prayer is short or long in time, I will boldly say that prayer is essential to one's life.

Prayer contains keys to life, which may unlock hidden treasures, that we may receive insight to the secret things of God.

In the mainstream of life, prayer invites God into our lives. This causes us to be dependent on God who created heaven and earth. Prayer can make us realize the need for God our Father in every part of our lives.

Deep Diving

Let us dive deep into the question, what is prayer?

Reflecting on the lifestyle of prayer, one can say that it is an intense and gratifying labor of love. Prayer is one of those blessed treasures of God that brings forth life to people and to situations that need a change – it is a promoter and generator of life. Why does prayer promote and generate life? Because we are talking with the Creator of life, this makes us partners with God – this is so amazing. Prayer is a conduit of the Kingdom of God, that is why we are commanded to pray without ceasing[5] This labor of love can cause an increase into our life and in the lives of others.

If prayer was not meant to be purposeful or intentional why would our Lord Jesus Christ instruct us to pray? In the Old Testament and as well as in the New Testament, there are illustrations of people who prayed and recorded results of their prayer life. Because of what was written in the Scriptures, which was for our learning[6], we are to pray with expectancy knowing that God hears and responds to our prayers. Again, prayer is a life-giving source.

Prayer is an act of worship. The Strong's Concordance defined worship as to prostrate oneself in homage (do reverence to adore). Settled in the scripture in John 4:23, Jesus said, *"But the hour is coming, and now is, when the true worshippers will worship the Father in spirit and truth; for the Father is seeking such to worship Him."* *'Father, may we pray to You in spirit and truth.'*

Prayer is our time with the Father, submitting ourselves in humility. Wycliffe defined humility as a mental attitude of lowliness. I Peter 5:5-7 *"Likewise you younger people, submit yourselves to your*

---

[5] Thessalonians 5:17
[6] Romans 15:4

elders. Yes, all of you be submissive to one another and be clothed with humility, for 'God resists the proud, but give grace to the humble.' Therefore, humble yourselves under the mighty hand of God that He may exalt you in due time, casting all your care upon Him, for He cares for you." 'Father, may we all bow our hearts as well as our knees to You with a heart of humility.'

Prayer is seeking God. Merriam-Webster Dictionary defined seeking as to search for; try to reach or obtain. The prophet David said it best in Psalm 42:1, *"As the deer pants for the water brooks, so pants my soul for You, O God."* The prophet also said in Psalm 63:1, *"O God, You are my God; early will I seek You; My soul thirsts for You; My flesh longs for You in a dry and thirsty land where there is no water."* 'Holy Spirit touch us that we may have a desire that is strong for God our Father.'

Prayer will help us not to enter temptation. In Luke 22:40, the Lord Jesus said to His disciples, *"Pray that you may not enter into temptation."* This is the place that we may exclaim what is written in I John 4:4, *"...He who is in you is greater than he who is in the world."* 'God, may we remain in a posture of prayer that we will not fall into the depths of temptation.' This verse does not say that we will not encounter temptation, but that prayer will help and strengthen us during the time that we are being tempted.

Prayer is an attitude of meshing our wills to the will of God. May we be one with the Father. Written in Luke 22:41-42, *"And He was withdrawn from them about a stone's throw, and He knelt down and prayed, saying, 'Father, if it is Your will, take this cup away from Me; nevertheless, not My will, but Yours be done.'"* This will be a glorious thing if we had an attitude like the Lord Jesus. 'Lord, we pray that Your will be done in the lives of Your children.'

Prayer helps in developing our faith. Luke 22:31-32, Jesus said,

"Simon, Simon! Indeed, Satan has asked for you, that he may sift you as wheat. But I have prayed for you, that your faith should not fail; and when you have returned to Me, strengthen your brethren."

Prayer creates the possibility of strengthening our hearts that we may not faint. Written in Luke 18:1 were the words of our Lord Jesus, *"Then He spoke a parable to them, that men always ought to pray and not loose heart."*

Prayer will enable our hearts to bow in repentance. The prophet's heart cry in Psalm 51:10 was that God would create in him a clean heart and renew a steadfast spirit within him. Let our heart's cry be the same, 'Lord please help me.'

Prayer gives us the ability to pray for those who persecute us. Matthew 5:44-45, *"But I say to you, love your enemies, bless those who curse you, do good to those who hate you, and pray for those who spitefully use you and persecute you, that you may be of your Father in heaven; for He makes His sun rise on the evil and on the good and sends rain on the just and on the unjust."* 'Father, I pray for those who spitefully use and persecute me.'

Prayer makes it possible to call out to our Helper. We can see this from the words of Jesus in John 14:16, *"And I will pray the Father, and He will give you another Helper, that He may abide with you forever."* 'Holy Spirit help us to pray.'

Prayer can put God in remembrance of His promises. Nehemiah from the Old Testament put God in remembrance to His word.

Nehemiah 5:19, *"Remember me, my God, for good, according to all that I have done for this people."*

Prayer will allow us to see the open Heaven. Luke 3:21, *"When all the people were baptized, it came to pass that Jesus also was baptized; and while He prayed, the heaven was open.*" May the Lord Jesus be our example.

May our foundation for prayer rest in Romans 8:26-27, "*Likewise the Spirit also helps in our weaknesses. For we do not know what we should pray for as we ought, but the Spirit Himself makes intercession for us with groanings which cannot be uttered. Now He who searches the hearts knows what the mind of the Spirit is, because He makes intercession for the saints according to the will of God.*"

Prayer connects earth to heaven that we may hear from God so that His will may spreads throughout all the earth. Take note: 2 Chronicles 7:14; "*If My people who are called by My name will humble themselves and pray and seek My face, and turn from their wicked ways, then I will hear from heaven and will forgive their sin and heal their land.*" The call is to reach heaven from the earth.

Basically speaking, prayer is an attitude of the heart which causes us to draw near to the One who loves and gave His Son for us. Prayer will cause our lives to intertwine with the heart of God.

The blessedness of prayer is that we have access to the Father, through our Lord Jesus Christ with the help of Holy Spirit. Our Lord gave instructions that we are to pray in His name, Mark 11:24, "Therefore I say to you, whatever things you ask when you pray, believe that you receive them, and you will have them." This is also written in John 14:13-14 and Colossians 3:17.

Because of the preciousness of prayer, Revelations 5: 8 bears repeating, "*Now when He had the scroll, the four living creatures and the twenty-four elders fell down before the Lamb, each having a harp and golden bowl full of incense, which are the prayers of the saints.*"

Our prayers are presented before God in golden vials.

What is your definition of prayer?

____

____

____

____

____

____

____

____

____

____

____

____

Are you intentional or purposeful while praying?

____

____

____

____

____

____

____

____

____

____

____

____

Why do we Pray?

The ultimate question, why do we pray, or is prayer necessary? Yes, the Scriptures have instructed us to pray—this will benefit our lives and the lives of others. Our closeness with God comes from prayer, studying and reading the Word of God—this is how we learn the characteristics of God, our Lord Jesus, and the Holy Spirit.

The first mentioned about praying (palal)-don't confuse this first occurrence of 'palal' with first occurrence of call - Genesis 20:7 *"Now therefore, restore the man's wife; for he is a prophet, and he will pray for you, and you shall live. But if you do not restore her, know that you shall surely die, you and all who are yours."*

Genesis 20:17, *"So Abraham prayed to God; and God healed Abimelech, his wife, and his female servants. Then they bore children; for the Lord had closed up all the wombs of the house of Abimelech because of Sarah, Abraham's wife."*

Because of prayer, God healed the King, his wife, and the King's servants.

In the Epistle of I Thessalonians 5:17 we are instructed to *"pray without ceasing."*

Recorded in the book of James 5:13-14, *"Is anyone among you suffering? Let him pray. Is anyone cheerful? Let him sing psalms. Is anyone among you sick? Let him call for the elders of the church and let them pray over him."*

James 5:15-16; *"And the prayer of faith will save the sick, and the Lord will raise him up. And if he has committed sins, he will be forgiven. Confess your trespasses to one another and pray for one another, that you may be healed. The effective, fervent prayer of a righteous man avails much."* The Christian Standard Bible has this verse written as this, *"The prayer of faith will save the sick person, and the Lord will raise him up; if he has committed sins, he will be forgiven. Therefore, confess your sins to one another and pray for one another, so that you may be healed. The prayer of a righteous person is very powerful in its effect."*

The result of prayer written in James 5:17-18, *"Elijah was a man with a nature like ours, and he prayed earnestly that it would not rain; and it did not rain on the land for three years and six months. And he prayed again, and the heaven gave rain, and the earth produced its fruit."* This is an illustration of the power of prayer.

Why pray? So that temptation may not have its way in our lives. Luke 22:40, *"When He came to the place, He said to them, "Pray that you may not enter into temptation."*

Recorded in Luke 22:31-32, *"And the Lord said, "Simon, Simon! Indeed, Satan has asked for you, that he may sift you as wheat. But I have prayed for you, that your faith should not fail; and when you have returned to Me, strengthen your brethren."*

In the Book of Acts 12:5, the saints prayed for Peter while he was in prison and the prison doors were open. *"Peter was therefore kept in prison, but constant prayer was offered to God for him by the church."* Why pray? At various times in our lives, we need doors open— prayer can open locked doors. Because of the *insistent* prayers of the saints' bolted jail cell doors were open for the Apostle Peter.

In Colossian 4:2; the Scripture states to *"continue earnestly in prayer, being vigilant in it with thanksgiving."* The Merriam-Webster Dictionary defined the following words: continue - to maintain without interruption; endure; to remain in a place or condition; earnestly - as grave important; vigilant - alertly watchful esp.to avoid danger.

The previous Scripture speaks volume—this verse pacts a mighty punch which employs the importance of having a persistent prayer life—staying in touch with the Father—to persevere in overcoming the power of distractions.

Paul wrote of being earnest in our prayer life, this is to teach us that prayers are of monumental importance. This is an admonition for us to never stop praying—no matter what the situation. Hopefully, we will not give up or be lackadaisical on something that is so valuable to our lives and the lives of others. The idea of being vigilant is to also be watchful. Are we watchful? We are to watch in the natural as well in the spirit realm. Luke 21:36 stated, *"Watch therefore and pray always that you may be counted worthy to escape all these things that will come to pass, and to stand before the Son of man."* What are all these things? They are the events of life.

How can one be watchful in the natural world? We can perform this task by being observant with the events that are surrounding us in our day to day living. There are all sorts of situations that are in our environment; some events are close encountered and other events are at a distance, but still happening all the same—these are great opportunities for prayer.

These watchful occurrences may include yourself, family members, neighbors, or someone just walking down the street. To be watchful is to be aware of prayer opportunities that are in your natural eyesight. This charge can really involve everyone; all we must do is see a need of someone. An event may take place while you are driving in your vehicle. You may see someone that has a need for prayer—at that point of time, you can pray about what you are witnessing to the Father, through Jesus Christ by the Holy Spirit.

Example: While driving you may see someone on the sidewalk that you may think is homeless. You can then pray, 'Father in the Name of Jesus bless that person.'

How can we be watchful in the spirit? This is a dying to self-task. A matter of saturation in the presence of our Holy Father. Our greatest example of watching in the spirit is our Lord Jesus Christ.

Let us define the word saturation. According to The Merriam-Webster Dictionary saturation is an adjective of saturate. Saturate – to soak thoroughly or to treat or charge with something to the point where no more can be absorbed, dissolved, or retained.

Can you imagine yourself saturated with the presence of God by the Lord Jesus Christ through the Holy Spirit?

The Scriptures has stated in I John 4:17: *"...because as He is, so are we in this world."*

Our Lord has given us a key throughout the Word of God. A key is His close communion in prayer with the Father. Throughout the Gospels, there are various recorded prayers of our Lord Jesus.

John 5:19: *"Then Jesus answered and said to them, 'Most assuredly, I say to you, the Son can do nothing of Himself, but what He sees the Father do; for whatever He does, the Son also does in like manner.'"* How can this be? By His close relationship with the Father.

The Lord Jesus was on the Earth and the Father in Heaven, so how could the Lord see what God saw and do what he did? Our Lord Jesus was seeing in the spiritual realm; therefore, He was watching in the spirit. This was not a natural transaction but spiritual one.

We must remember that God our Father is a Spirit (John 4:24). So how can we see what the Father sees and do what the Father does? This can happen through the blessed Holy Spirit. The Lord said in John 16:7; *"Nevertheless I tell you the truth. It is to your advantage that I go away; for if I do not go away, the Helper will not come to you; but if I depart, I will send Him to you."* Well, our Lord is seated at the right hand of the Father (Hebrews 1:3) and the Holy Spirit is here with us. John 16:13; *"However, when He, the Spirit of truth, has come, He will guide you into all truth; for He will not speak on His own authority, but whatever He hears He will speak; and He will tell you things to come." "He will glorify Me, for he will take of what is Mine and declare it to you."*

'Father, may we see as You see and do what You do.'

Why pray? So that the gospel may spread throughout all the Earth. 2 Thessalonians 3:1, *"Finally, brethren, pray for us, that the word of the Lord may run swiftly and be glorified, just as it is with you."*

Why pray? Prayer is honoring God by submitting ourselves and being humble to Him. Prayer aligns our lives with the Father in Heaven. It will also help to keep the enemy at bay. Having a prayer life uplifts the name of Jesus Christ and will give Him honor. There are various reasons why we pray, and each reason is beneficial to our lives and to the lives of others. Through our life of prayer, may we draw close to God, that our hearts desire is one with His heart's desire and to have His will perfected in us.

The Scriptures bear witness that we must remain in a posture of prayer.

Saints of God, may we realize that prayer is a guiding light throughout our lifetime. May our heart's cry be, 'Father we want to know You.'

What are your reasons for praying?

Our Loving Father

Our Father's abode is in this place called Heaven; He has an all-seeing eye upon His children—which makes Him truly a present help in the time of trouble.[7] God knows about the many troubles before they enter our lives, but He said in His Word, that He has made a way of escape for us.[8]

Written in Luke 12:7; *"But the very hairs of your head are numbered…"* Why would the Holy Spirit have Luke the physician to inscribe about the number of hairs that are on our heads? So that we may know how precious we are to God and nothing about us is insignificant to the Father who is in heaven. Yes, you and I are prized possessions to our loving Father—He gave His only begotten Son, Jesus Christ, to die on the cross on our behalf and raised from the dead on the third day that we may have life eternal with God the Father.

Heaven is God's throne room which exhibits His Sovereignty and authority—our place on earth connects us to His abiding place—this gives us an uninterrupted channel of communication with God our Father and to receive His expressions of love. There is no time or season presented to man where he cannot have access to God through our Lord Jesus Christ by the Holy Spirit.

He is above all our trials that invades our life; God declares our end from the beginning.[9] Because of His ever living-presence, may we realize and have an understanding heart to know that we can trust and rest in the bosom of our heavenly Father.

Our God sees everywhere and everything all at the same time—His vision does not have any obstructions. This is evident in Psalm

[7] Psalm 46:1
[8] I Corinthians 10:13
[9] Isaiah 46:10

139:1-2, *"O Lord, You have searched me and known me. You know my sitting down and my rising up; You understand my thought afar off."*

Some earthly fathers do the best they can in their children's lives, but there is still no comparison to our Father in Heaven. Some fathers have abandoned their children; our heavenly Father will never leave us nor forsake us.[10] Some fathers, at the best of their ability, try to understand their children, but this Father in Heaven knew us before the foundation of the world.

Some fathers do not have a relationship with their children or desire to have a relationship with the ones that they brought into this life, but this Father in Heaven has an everlasting love for His children.

Imagine that the God of all creativity desires to have us in His family. We are a family under the submissiveness of the ever-loving God.

Written in the Scriptures is that God sent His only begotten Son to an unregenerated world—so that we may know that His desire is for us to be with Him throughout all eternity— John 3:16, *"For God so loved the world that He gave His only begotten Son, that whoever believes in Him should not perish but have everlasting life."*

Yes, we were sinners; He sent the Lord Jesus to conquer our sin nature so that we can become a part of His family.[11] Written in the Gospel of John 1:12-13; *"But as many as received Him, to them He gave the right to become children of God, to those who believe in His name: who were born, not of blood, nor of the will of the flesh, nor of the will of man, but of God"*—we are adopted in the family of God.[12]

---

[10] Hebrews 13:5
[11] Romans 8:4
[12] Ephesians 1:5

God has adopted us as believers with all our faults and disappointments—we were so loved that we were chosen. Love has adopted us and has chosen us to be His children in His kingdom. There is no greater love for us than the love of the Father in Heaven. He is available for us to talk and walk with Him. This God, our Father will never leave nor abandon us. When we think of the Father in Heaven, may we think about this great love.

Jesus is the head of the family of God, and He will never die, get sick or get feeble. In our older years, we sometime must change places with our parent(s) to become caretakers of them, written in the Word of God is that *Jesus is the same yesterday, today, and forever more.*[13] *He will never change, so we can always trust Him.* There will never be any blindness in His eyes, this Father will always be able to see us. There will never be any deadness in His heart—His love is everlasting. There will never be any hearing loss; our Father will always hear our prayers. This Father in heaven has borne us into His family. Oh yes, we are in the family of God. May we recognize our connection with one another because we are joint heirs with His beloved Son, Jesus Christ.[14]

Beloved just as Jesus is, so are we in this world - I John 4:17.

---

[13] Hebrews 13:8
[14] Romans 8:17

Teach us to Pray

Luke 11:1

Instructions on Prayer

Oxford Language Dictionary defined 'instructions' as: 1. Direction or order. 2. Detailed information telling how something should be done, operated, or assembled.

In Mathew 6:5-7, the Lord has given us explicit instructions on prayer. These instructions are included in the famous sermon known as the Sermon on the Mount that introduced to the world what is referred to as the well-known 'Beatitudes.'

According to the Merriam-Webster Dictionary, beatitude means the state of utmost bliss, also defined as supreme blessedness. In other words, our Lord is teaching us how to walk in the supreme blessedness through prayer which is a conduit to obtaining a life of contentment, no matter what our life situations may dictate to us.

Matthew 6:5-8:

"And when you pray, you shall not be like the hypocrites. For they love to pray standing in the synagogues and on the corners of the streets, that they may be seen by men. Assuredly, I say to you, they have their reward. "But you, when you pray, go into your room, and when you have shut your door, pray to your Father who is in the secret place; and your Father who sees in secret will reward you openly. And when you pray, do not use vain repetitions as the heathen do. For they think that they will be heard for many words. Therefore, do not be like them. For your Father knows the things you have need of before you ask Him."

Our Lord did not leave anything to our imagination or to our own reasoning. We do not have to guess how the Lord wanted us to pray. When we follow the Lord's instructions, then we will not lean to our own understanding.

"When you Pray"

Matthew 6:5, *"And when you pray……"*

Highlighting the above statement, we can see how the Lord detailed the importance of prayer. May we take note that He did not make this a conditional statement, but said *"and when you pray,"* giving the understanding that in our Christian walk there is no room for not having a prayer life—engaging in personal time with the Lord.

Our prayer life can lead to a state of happiness, well-being or comfort within our hearts and minds hidden in the love of God. Beloved, prayer gives us the privilege of having an abiding relationship with the Father by the Lord Jesus Christ and through the Holy Spirit, which will affect our lives.

Prayer is the place where we can find contentment, peace, receive the love of the Father, instructions for our day, purpose for life, this list can go on and on. Prayer being a divine relationship with the Father which depicts our dependence on God. May we pray to get guidance from the Master.

Realizing prayer is holy communication. Why? Because we are engaged in conversation with the Holy One of heaven and earth who is the designer and giver of life. The designer and giver of life loves us and desires us to draw near to Him. Oh, what an honor to pray to God our Father!

God our Father sees all and knows all—so it is to our benefit to seek His face in prayer. Prayer is a bridge from Earth to Heaven, so that we may receive from Heaven to Earth. Hopefully, we will see the need for prayer and the delight in praying.

Prayer is a team effort with God—and mind you, this is a winning team.

'Thank You Lord Jesus for making this possible by giving us the means to fellowship with God and to have the desire that the Holy Spirit will manifest God's presence and His will in our lives.'

'Thank You Father God for offering the opportunity to pray to You and thank You for the blessedness of being intimate with You. May we hear Your voice to enlighten our minds that Your will be lived out in our lives.'

One of the purposes of prayer is to have the Kingdom of God manifested in our lives while living on this planet. In our ignorance we think prayer is to only benefit us. Prayer is also requesting that we perform His will and purpose while living on this earth. The will of God benefits eternity which includes us.

While engaged in prayer, we are to praise, thank, acknowledge, and worship His Holiness. We are to recognize and express His greatness while in a posture of prayer. Our God is worthy of praise in His awesomeness. Written in Psalms 93:1; *"...the Lord is clothed with strength, wherewith he hath girded Himself."* We are to praise and worship the God of gods and the King of kings.

May we have Him first in our prayer life.

The Lord Jesus is the greatest example to model our prayer life. He often withdrew Himself away from the crowd and His disciples to commune with His Father.

Note the following prayer postures of the Lord.

Matthew 14:23: *"And when He had sent the multitudes away, He went up on the mountain by Himself to pray."* Prayer was so important to the Lord Jesus that He left the multitude to commune with the Father.

Matthew 19:13: *"Then little children were brought to Him that He might put His hands on them and pray, but the disciples rebuked them."* The disciples thought it would be best to give a stern correction to the children and their parents, but the Lord thought it better that He would pray for the children, and He compared the children to the Kingdom of Heaven.

Matthew 26:36: *"Then Jesus came with them to a place called Gethsemane, and said to the disciples, 'Sit here while I go and pray over there.'"* The Lord was troubled and had turmoil in His Spirit, but during His time of anguish, He turned to the Father in prayer. May we have the heart to do the same and turn to the Father in our time of need.

Mark 1:35, *"Now in the morning, having risen a long while before daylight, He went out and departed to a solitary place; and there He prayed."* Oh, the desire to be alone with the Father. Connecting with God before the start of the busyness of the day. Written in Psalms 118:24, *"This is the day that the Lord has made…"* Since the Lord made the day, may we begin our day with the One who has made it.

Luke 3:21, *"When all the people were baptized, it came to pass that Jesus also was baptized; and while He prayed, the heaven was opened."* 'Father when we pray, may we recognize that Heaven is already open.'

Luke 5:16, *"So He Himself often withdrew into the wilderness and prayed."* May we draw away to be alone with the Father and commit ourselves to Him in prayer.

Luke 6:12, *"Now it came to pass in those days that He went out to the mountain to pray and continued all night in prayer to God."* At times, we must remain in God's face until we know the answer.

Luke 9: 28-29, *"Now it came to pass, about eight days after these sayings, that He took Peter, John, and James and went up on the mountain to pray. As He prayed, the appearance of His face was altered, and His robe became white and glistening."* 'Father help us to remain in Your presence until our countenance is changed.'

Luke 22:32, *"But I have prayed for you, that your faith should not fail, and when you have returned to Me, strengthen your brethren."* Prayer is the foundation for our faith not to faulter because without prayer we will succumb to temptation.

John 14:16, *"And I will pray the Father and He will give you another Helper, that He may abide with you forever."* 'Holy Spirit, would You lead and guide us through the day.'

John 16:26, *"In that day you will ask in My name, and I do not say to you that I shall pray the Father for you;"* 'Thank You Lord Jesus that You have made it possible for us to come to the Father because the Father loves and desires us to commune with Him.'

As written in the Epistle of 1 John 4:17, *"....as He is, so are we in this world."* Our Lord Jesus was a man of prayer and was committed to prayer. May we as the people of God try to reach this same goal in our lives. Again, *....as He is, so are we in this world."*

'Thank You, Lord Jesus, for showing us the way.'

How can you improve on your prayer life?

Watch your moral Compass

Matthews 6:5

"..., you shall not be like the hypocrites. For they love to pray standing in the synagogues and on the corners of the streets, that they may be seen by men. Assuredly, I say to you, they have their reward."

The Wycliffe Dictionary defined hypocrites as being in the context of Greek drama, the term hypocrite was applied to an actor on the theater state. Since an actor pretends to be someone other than himself, *hypocrite* was applied metaphorically to a person who "acts a part" in real life, pretending to be better than he is, one who simulates goodness.

The Holman Bible dictionary defined hypocrisy as pretense to being what one really is not, especially the pretense of being a better person than one really is.

Why do we pray or who is our audience when we pray? Do we pray for the recognition of men or God?

Imagining yourself in a prayer group, holding hands in a circle of approximately fifteen people. The request is for everyone in the group to pray. Here comes the heart palpitations and sweaty hands. Thoughts racing in one's head. What am I to say? How will I sound to the other fourteen people? Oh, my turn is coming up! The others sounded good; will I be able to pray like them?

The above paragraph is the likelihood; this has happened to a great deal of us. Do we realize to whom we are praying? I believe we all have heard on various occasions people boasting on someone else's prayer and quietly wishing to be able to pray the same way. From whom is the reward coming? Is it man or God—are we to receive accolades from men regarding our conversation with God?

<u>True Story:</u> On my job we had Bible Study during our lunch time. On a certain day, two women were substituting for one of the Bible teachers. While listening to them teach and pray, I was amazed at how they taught the Scriptures and prayed. After work, driving home, I was pondering on what I witnessed during the Bible study. When we reached one of the destinations (we were in a carpool), we parked and waited for one of the carpool members to come from their parents' home. When alone, I began to talk to the Lord about what I observed during the Bible study and tears began to flow from my eyes. Then I said to the Lord, "I could not teach or pray like those two women"; they were full of power. After talking to the Lord and wiping my tears from my face, the sister of one of the carpool members came from their parents' home and said, "Mommy said to give you this flower." It was a green potted plant of white lilies. At that moment, my heart was calm and peaceful. I then realized that the Lord did not want me to be like those two women or anyone. However, when we pray, whether it is loud, soft spoken, teaching or preaching, it is to the Lord.

In Matthew 6:5, the Lord has cautioned us to watch our motives when we pray and not to be like the hypocrites.

We must learn to be intentional and recognize to whom we are addressing in our prayer. It is so easy to want affirmation from our peers seeking to know how we sound and if the prayer was correct. What is the correct prayer? The correct prayer is the prayer from our hearts.

The Lord Jesus spoke about the person who prays in a hypocritical manner wants to be seen of men, looking for recognition from people.

The question for all of us to ask ourselves is to whom are we praying, and does the Lord hear our prayer?

How is your heart when you pray?

Recorded in Luke 18:9-14 is a parable spoken by the Lord regarding a pharisee who trusted in himself and thought that he was having prayer time with God. This pharisee compared himself with a tax collector and thought himself to be righteous and the tax collector to be unrighteous.

We cannot judge someone else's heart, especially while the person is praying to God. The Bible stated that these two men went to the temple to pray. But the religious man concerned himself with the tax collector. Beloved God knew about the tax collector, pharisee and He also knows about us. The pharisee approached God with pride by exalting himself and the tax collector approached God with humility.

Approaching God with humility is a sure way to get His attention. Our Father is the only One who can judge the heart of any human being.

The Holman Bible Dictionary defined humility as a personal quality in which an individual shows dependence on God and respect for others.

The Wycliffe Bible Dictionary defined humility a Christian characteristic. Humility is a mental attitude of lowliness, the opposite of pride. It is a specific grace developed in the Christian by the Spirit of God wherein the believer frankly acknowledges that all he has and is he owes to the Triune God who is dynamically operative in his behalf.

'Father, would You create a clean heart and renew a right spirit within us.'[15]

---

[15] Psalm 51:10

How can you make improvements with your attitude?

Intimacy with the Father

Matthews 6:6

"But you, when you pray, go into your room, and when you have shut your door, pray to your Father who is in the secret place, and your Father who sees in secret will reward you openly."

Again, the call is to pray, and the Lord gave instructions on where to pray. The Lord said, *"Go into your room and shut the door."* What is the purpose of going into your room and shutting the door? When we enter our room or closet to shut the door and pray, this is absolute privacy with God, which shuts out everything beyond the closed door. This is personal and intimate time with God. He made it known that the Father is in secret and sees in secret but will reward us openly.

According to the Strong's Exhaustive Concordance, the Greek word for closet is 'tameion', i.e., a chamber on the ground-floor or interior of an Oriental house generally used for storage or privacy.

Holman Bible Dictionary – A private room in a dwelling where Jesus encouraged people to pray (Matt. 6:6). He also noted that not even words said in the inner room privacy could be kept secret (Luke12:3), indicating the pharisees' hypocrisy could not be hidden. A biblical closet is an actual room, not a storage place.

Wycliffe – The NT stresses the ideas of privacy, even secrecy, and storage, as suggested in the terms store chamber, upper chamber, secret chamber, inner room, and private room.

Zondervan Illustrated Bible Dictionary – private room, inner chamber.

According to the Strong's Concordance – the Greek word for secret is 'krupto' – defined as concealed i.e., private, hidden.

The instruction is to go into your hidden place. The Lord has made it known that all who pray should have a secret place or a special place—this place is designed for only God and you— all else is to be on the outside of the closet. I call this the birthing place.

(Please note that a secret place does not have to be a literal closet or a room with a closed door—but a certain place where you have your prayer time with the Father.)

Why is this secret place so important? This is the place of intimacy with God—even though we may be interceding for others–this creates a close union with God. In this quiet place we may get to know the heart of the Father. The secret place is where secrets are disclosed between God and you. We come to Him in secret, and He rewards us openly. Psalm 91:1: *"He who dwells in the secret place of the Most High shall abide under the shadow of the Almighty."*

In the Strong's Concordance, the Greek word for open is 'phaneoros' defined as apparent, publicly, manifest. The open place allows for the manifestation of the reward.

John 5:19; *"Then Jesus answered and said to them, 'Most assuredly, I say to you, the Son can do nothing of Himself, but what He sees the Father do; for whatever He does, the Son also does in like manner. For the Father loves the Son, and shows Him all things that He Himself does; and He will show Him greater works than these, that you may marvel...'"*

How can this be, when His Father is in Heaven and our Lord on the Earth? How did He see what the Father saw and do what the Father did? All this took place in the secret closet. May we get into that secret place and see what the Father sees and do what the Father does. 'Holy Spirit, please help us.'

The close union with the Father will unveil itself in our lives.

We see in various Scriptures how the Lord went away from the crowd and His disciples to be alone to commune with God. May we purpose in our hearts to make alone time with the Father in Heaven.

The reward from God is the answer to prayer.

One of the great men of the Bible was the servant of God, Moses. His time alone with the Lord on the mountain top resulted with the Law of God. Referenced in the Christian Study Bible in Exodus 24:1-2, *"Then He said to Moses, 'Go up to the Lord, you, and Aaron, Nadab, and Abihu, and seventy of Israel's elders, and bow in worship at a distance. Moses alone is to approach the Lord, but the others are not to approach the Lord, and the people are not to go up with him.'"*

Meditate on Exodus 33:11; *"So the Lord spoke to Moses' face to face, as a man speaks to his friend. And he would return to the camp, but his servant Joshua the son of Nun, a young man, did not depart from the tabernacle."* Because of his intimate time with the Father, Joshua became a great warrior for the army of God.

One of my favorite servants in the Scripture is the man after God's heart who was King David (I Samuel 13:14). Before he became king, he often communed alone with God. This is seen in Psalm 142(KJV), *"I cried unto the Lord with my voice, with my voice unto the Lord did I make my supplication. I poured out my complaint before him. I shewed him my trouble. ..."*

Of course, we can turn our attention to Daniel 6:10: *"Now when Daniel knew that the writing was signed, he went home. And in his upper room, with his windows open toward Jerusalem, he knelt down on his knees three times that day, and prayed and gave thanks before his God, as was his custom since the early days."*

We can see the precious oil from these men's lives from having the special one on one time with the Father. This secret place has great rewards.

Depicted throughout the Bible are variations of prayer. Prayer can be private as well as public. The reference in Matthew 6:6 is about private prayer.

The invitation is to come to the Father. Slip away to the secret place, away from the noise and the various life distractions that always need our attention. In the Book of Revelations 4:1......" And the first voice which I heard was like a trumpet speaking with me, saying, "*Come up here, and I will show you things which must take place after this*" '*Do we also hear the call to come?*'

Steal away.

The time you spend in prayer, has it affected your life?

Vain Repetitions

Matthew 6:7

"And when you pray, do not use vain repetitions as the heathen do. For they think that they will be heard for their many words."

According to the Strong's Concordance, the Greek word for vain repetition is 'battalogeo' which means to prate tediously. Merriam-Webster Dictionary defined prate as to talk long and idly, chatter foolishly.

Also, the Strong's Concordance defined heathen as to mean Gentile. Gentile is a person who is outside of the Jewish community.

Our Lord is not speaking against repetitive prayers, but prayers that are empty without any substance. Vain repetitions are prayers without purpose or faith. When we come to God, may we be intentional and having our hearts to love on Him.

The intent may be of worship, thanksgiving, intercession, petition, supplication, etc. When we come to the Father, may we have a purpose or a reason for coming. What are we expecting from God when we come to Him? Are we expecting Him to receive our worship, are we expecting Him to receive our prayer when we come to Him in the act of intercession?

After we pray, do we say in our hearts, 'well I have done my duty for today'? Do we realize this is a real conversation with the One who has created all things?

Vain repetitions are repetitive prayers without belief—routine prayers—are we coming to Him out of formality or habit? Are our prayers dutiful or purposeful? What is the intent for praying?

We can see this lived out in I Kings 18:29: "...*And when midday was past, they prophesied until the time of the offering of the evening sacrifice. But there was no voice; no one answered, no one paid attention.*" The events are still happening today, coming before God with our own traditions with the voidance of faith.

Hebrews 11:6, "*But without faith it is impossible to please Him, for he who comes to God must believe that He is, and that He is a rewarder of those who diligently seek Him.*"

I John 5:14-15, "*Now this is the confidence that we have in Him, that if we ask anything according to His will, He hears us. And if we know that He hears us, whatever we ask, we know that we have the petitions that we have asked of Him.*"

Our prayers are spiritual transactions.

Recorded in the Christian Standard Bible. James 5:16; "*Therefore, confess your sins to one another and pray for one another, so that you may be healed. The prayer of a righteous person is very powerful in its effect.*"

In the previous verse, the command is to confess our sins and to pray one for another. In this verse the reason for the prayer is healing. The spiritual transaction is confession and prayer; then receive the healing.

Question, is your prayer life ritualistic or purposeful?

In prayer, may the love of God smother our hearts, through our Lord Jesus by the Holy Spirit. Let the spiritual transaction be one of love from the Father—to the Father.

Have you ever prayed in vain? If so, when, and how did you make corrections?

The Father Knows

Matthew 6:8

"Therefore, do not be like them. For your Father knows the things you have need of before you ask Him...."

The Lord made a statement, "Do not be like them." The question may arise, who are we not to emulate. The answer is the Gentiles – in this instance meaning those who are outside of the sonship of God.

Our prayers are not to try to manipulate the Father or to try pressure God into doing something.

As referenced in Mathew 7:9-11, *"Or what man is there among you who, if his son asks for bread, will give him a stone? Or if he asks for a fish, will he give him a serpent? If you then, being evil (natural), know how to give good gifts to your children, how much more will your Father who is in heaven give good things to those who ask Him!?"*

We do not have to beg but to entreat.

Written in Jeremiah 65:24, *"It shall come to pass that before they call, I will answer; and while they are still speaking, I will hear."*

Philippians 4:19, *"And my God shall supply all you need according to His riches in glory by Christ Jesus."*

The Father knows what we have need of.

Do you realize that the Father knows everything about you?

In This Manner

Matthew 6:9-13, *"In this manner, therefore, pray."*

According to the Strong's Concordance the Greek word for manner is 'houto/houtos' defined as to precede or follow.

Merriam-Webster Dictionary defined manner as 1. kind, sort; 2. a way of acting or proceeding; 3. a method of artistic execution; 4. social conduct; 5. behavior

"Our Father in heaven, Hallowed be Your name. Your kingdom come. Your will be done on earth as it is in heaven. Give us this day our daily bread. And forgive us our debts, as we forgive our debtors. And do not lead us into temptation but deliver us from the evil one. For Yours is the kingdom and the power and the glory forever. Amen."

The above model prayer depicts several characteristics that the Lord would have us to incorporate in our prayers, below are listed eleven of the characteristics.

Relationship
Honoring God's Name
God's Kingdom
God's Will
On earth as in heaven
Provision
Forgiveness
Temptation
Deliverance
Kingdom, Power, and Glory
Amen

Relationship

Lord, Teach us to Pray

Matthews 6:9(a)

"Our Father in Heaven."

Do not ignore this small three letter word.

Our

This small three letter word "Our" in the beginning of the model prayer has a great influence over the following verses of the prayer.

According to GRAMMAR?, the word 'Our' is a plural possessive determiner that means "belonging to us."

Merriam-Webster Dictionary defined 'Our' as of or relating to us or ourselves or ourself, especially as possessors or possessor, agents or agent, or objects or object of an action. The New Edition of the Merriam-Webster Dictionary defined 'Our' as of relating to us or ourselves. The Oxford Languages defined 'Our' as belonging to or associated with the speaker and one or more other people previously mentioned or easily identified; and used by a writer, editor, or monarch to refer to something belonging to or associated with himself or herself.

May we agree or acknowledge that the 'Our' in this prayer has made a correlation that God is our Father which denotes family. Rest on the understanding that the Lord Jesus did not say my Father or your Father (meaning the disciples), but *our* Father which gave credence that we are the family of God—a household of God.

Let us meditate on the fact that the Lord Jesus instructed us to go into our room or secret place of intimacy to spend time with the Father. Yet in this place of intimacy, the Lord would have us to think and pray for others. We are told to include others in our prayers by the command 'Our'.

The Lord Jesus has given us the mindset of oneness.

This family of God is the Body of Christ which is also known as the church—not many churches—but the one church. May our hearts be enlarged to include others in our daily prayers that the great divide may be closed, and we are unified.

Can you imagine yourself in that intimate place with God and praying for the entire body of Christ?

Ephesians 6:18: *"Praying always with all prayer and supplication in the Spirit being watchful to this end with all perseverance and supplication for all the saints."*

To think of the many as the one-unity.

I Corinthians 12:12: *"For as the body is one and has many members, but all the members of the one body, being many, are one body, so also is Christ."*

Colossians 1:17-18: *"And He is before all things, and in Him all things consist. And He is the head of the body, the church, who is the beginning, the firstborn from the dead, that in all things He may have the preeminence."*

Brothers and sisters, take note of the previous scriptures, referencing the one body and the church, not speaking of many bodies and many churches, but only the one.

Consider the mind of God on the thought of unity.

Psalm 133:1-3: *"Behold, how good and how pleasant it is for brethren to dwell together in unity! It is like the precious oil upon the head, running down on the beard, the beard of Aaron, running down on the edge of his garments. It is like the dew of Hermon, descending upon the mountains of Zion; for there the Lord commanded the blessing – Life forevermore."*

'Lord, would You widen our vision that we may have a heart to pray as You would have us to pray.'

Father

Oxford Language's definition of relationship as the way in which two or more concepts, objects, or people are connected, or the state of being connected.

Father - In the Strong's Concordance, the Greek Word for Father is 'Pater,' meaning the male parent. Amos 3:3: *"Can two walk together, unless they are agreed? Leviticus 26:12: "I will walk among you and be your God, and you shall be My people."*

The HELPS Word-studies defined 'Pater'(father) as of our heavenly Father. He imparts life, from physical birth to the gift of eternal life through the second birth (regeneration, being born again). Through ongoing sanctification, the believer increasingly resembles their heavenly Father—i.e., each time they receive faith from Him and obey it, which results in their unique glorification.

The Aramaic Word for Father is 'Abba.' Galatians 4:6: *"...and because you are sons, God has sent for the Spirit of His Son into, your hearts, crying out, Abba, Father!"*

The Holman Bible Dictionary defined 'Abba' as the Aramaic Word for "father" used by Jesus to speak of His own intimate relationship with God, a relationship that others can enter through faith.

The Vines Expository of Dictionary Biblical Words defined Father as "a nourisher, protector, upholder" ...metaphorically, of the originator of a family or company of persons animated by the same spirit as himself, as of Abraham...

Zondervan Illustrated Bible Dictionary defined God as Father as Creator of the universe, "the Father of the heavenly lights" (Jas 1:17); as Creator of humans, *"Have we not all one father?"* (Mal 2:10): *As one who begets and takes care of his spiritual children, "You received the Spirit of sonship. And by him we cry, 'Abba, Father'"* (Rom.8:15). See Abba. In a special and unique sense, God is the Father of Jesus Christ (Matt 11:26; Mk 14:36; Lk. 22:42).

We are in a relationship with the Father above who is a nurturer of His people.

I John 3:1-2, *"Behold what manner of love the Father has bestowed on us, that we should be called children of God! Therefore, the world does not know us, because it did not know Him. Beloved, now we are children of God; and it has not yet been revealed what we shall be, but we know that when He is revealed, we shall be like Him, for we shall see Him as He is."*

Yes, beloved we shall see Him as He is because we are the children of God and belong to Him whose abode is in Heaven. What an honor to have the Creator of this world to be our heavenly Father.

What is a father? One who loves, cares, provides, nurtures, and can manage every situation that comes into his child's life; more importantly he is the one who has brought forth life—the one who has planted the seed that we may come forth into being.

In the Gospel of John 3:3; *"Jesus answered and said to him, most assuredly, I say to you, unless one is born again, he cannot see the kingdom of God."*

The Lord also said, in the Gospel of John 4:23-24, *"But the hour is coming, and now is, when the true worshipers will worship the Father in spirit and truth; for the Father is seeking such to worship Him. God is Spirit, and those who worship Him must worship in spirit and truth."*

In connection with these two previous Scriptures, may our hearts, souls, and minds be enlightened by knowing that God is Spirit. If we are born again, which means to be born from above (Heaven), then we too are spirit, in which we are spiritually alive to be who He would have us to be—Spirit to spirit. Being born from above is our bond with our heavenly Father and has given us the power to be sons of God because we are born of His Spirit. Written in the Gospel of John 1:12; *"But as many as received Him, to them He gave the right to become children of God, to those who believe in*

His name who were born, not of blood, nor of the will of the flesh, nor of the will of man, but of God."

Beloved brothers and sisters being born from above is a heavenly predetermination to bring us into the family of God—He has purposefully brought us forth into His kingdom. Because of the grace of God, Love has called us into love. Romans 8:29: *"For whom He foreknew, He also predestined to be conformed to the image of His Son, that He might be the firstborn among many brethren."*

What manner of love has the Father bestowed upon His children? May we receive this love described in Romans 8:38-39, *"For I am persuaded that neither death nor life, nor angels nor principalities nor powers, nor things present nor things to come, nor height nor depth, nor any other created thing, shall be able to separate us from the love of God, which is in Christ Jesus, our Lord."*

The Bible informs us about God's steadfast love, Psalm, 36:7, *"How precious is Your steadfast love, O God! The children of mankind take refuge in the shadow of Your wings."* Written in Jeremiah 31:3, *"The Lord appeared to him far away. I have loved you with an everlasting love; therefore, I have continued my faithfulness to you."* **Great is God's unfailing love for us.**

The promise of God to His children written in 2 Corinthians 6:18, *"I will be a Father to you, and you shall be My sons and daughters, Says the Lord Almighty."*

Our Father who is in Heaven is the God of gods, the Lord of lords, and Father above fathers and has chosen to love us and to be our Father. Our Father whose abode is in Heaven loves us.

How is your relationship with the Father, through the Lord Jesus, and by the Holy Spirit?

Honoring God's Name

Matthews: 6:9(b)

"Hallowed be Your Name."

The Strong's Concordance defined Hallowed as to consecrate; to venerate.

Merriam-Webster Dictionary expounded venerate as to regard with reverential respect.

According to the Strong's Concordance the Greek word for name is 'onoma' specified as authority, character.

Wycliffe Dictionary – Declaring one's name was a chief means of revealing or manifesting oneself.

The Christian Standard Bible recorded the above verse as *"Your name be honored as holy."*

Why do we hallow His name? **Because God is holy, and we are to worship Him in His Holiness.**

Isaiah 6:3: *"Holy, holy, holy is the Lord of hosts; The whole earth is full of His glory!"*

Psalm 96:6-9 declared the majesty of God, *"Honor and majesty are before Him; strength and beauty are in His sanctuary. Give to the Lord, O families of the peoples, Give to the Lord glory and strength. Give to the Lord, the glory due to His name; Bring an offering and come into His courts. Oh, worship the Lord in the beauty of holiness!"*

Revelations 4:8,11, *"...Holy, holy, holy, Lord God Almighty, Who was and is and is to come!... You are worthy, O Lord, to receive glory and honor and power; For You created all things, And by Your will they exist and were created."*

How glorious is our Lord!

The Scriptures declared the holiness of God's name.

Psalm 30:4, *"Sing praise to the Lord, you saints of His, and give thanks at the remembrance of His holy name."*

Psalm 97:12: *"Rejoice in the Lord, you righteous, and give thanks at the remembrance of His name."*

Proverbs 18:10: *"The name of the Lord is a strong tower; the righteous run to it and are safe."*

According to the Strong's Concordance, the Hebrew word for strong is 'oz'; (force, security, majesty, praise): boldness, loud, might, power, strength, strong. The Hebrew name for tower, 'migdal', 'mig: delah'; a tower (from its size or height - castle, flower, tower). Hebrew name for righteous, 'tsaddiyq'; just, lawful. Hebrew name for run, 'ruwts'; to rush.

The Bible declares in Romans 10:13, *"For whoever calls on the name of the LORD shall be saved."*

The Lord is giving us His name as a way of revealing Himself to us. What need is in your life—run to the strong tower that is greater than everyone, anything, and everything?

God is our present help in a time of need.[16] Even though He is our present help for any situation that may land in our lives, we are to reverence His name. Come before Him recognizing Him as Father, likewise for any parent(s) we are to give them respect. In prayer,

---

[16] Psalm 46:1

when we come to our Father in heaven, we are to honor His holy name.

In the Gospel of John 17:26, our Lord Jesus said, *"And I have declared to them Your name, and will declare it, that the love with which You loved Me may be in them, and I in them."*

Referenced in the above Scripture, the Lord has declared God's name, which revealed the attributes and characteristics of God. In turn may we make known our Father's wonderful qualities to those who may not know Him. Prayer enhances our relationship with the Father by the Lord Jesus, and through the Holy Spirit by giving us a deeper understanding of the Written Word.

We are to reverence the name of God—Hallowed be Your name.

He Is.

In what ways do you give God glory?

In what ways do you give God glory?

God's Kingdom

Matthew 6:10:

"Your Kingdom come."

The Kingdom of God is God's rule and reigning in our lives and on this earth.

What is meant by the Kingdom of God to come?

When praying for God's Kingdom to come, we are requesting that God's presence and His way of life to be obvious in the lives of His people.

Requesting God's Kingdom to come has a two-fold purpose. One purpose was to fulfill His way through His people while living on this earth and the other is to intreat God for the second advent of Jesus Christ. In this book, we are focusing on God's way of life to be apparent in the lives of His children. In short, it is our prayer request to manifest God's rule through His people while on earth.

Lamentations 5:16; *"You, O Lord, remain forever; Your throne from generation to generation."*

Strong's Concordance defined kingdom as royalty, rule, or a realm and the Greek word is 'basileia'.

The Holman Dictionary defined the Kingdom of God as God's kingly rule or sovereignty, which is the rule of God that is independent of all geographical areas or political entities. The kingdom was the rule of God which He extended over human lives through the ministry of Jesus, and it also is His rule which will be consummated or made complete in the future.

Wycliffe Dictionary – Passages in the epistles reveal that the rule of God on Earth today is effective only among those who have been delivered from darkness and transferred into the kingdom of His Son (Col 1:13). The kingdom exists at present where Christians are living in subject to the will of God, where His power is producing changed lives.

The Zondervan Illustrated Bible Dictionary defined the kingdom of God as a contemporary English, the word kingdom most commonly refers to the realm or territorial unit over which a monarch reigns, including the people that are under the monarch's rule. Fundamentally, however, the kingdom of God is His sovereign activity as King in saving sinners and overcoming evil. When we seek God's kingdom and righteousness, we seek God's rule in our lives (Matt 6:33). God's kingdom is, of course, not merely an abstract rule, but rather a dynamic force manifested in Christ to destroy His (spiritual) enemies and to bring to men and women the blessings of God's reign.

The Kingdom of God is mentioned in the Gospel of Luke thirty-two times and fourteen times in the Gospel of Mark. According to the Holman Dictionary, the Lord Jesus made the kingdom of God central in His preaching and more than a hundred references to the kingdom appear in the gospels.

Those who are in the family of God have a dual citizenship—one of the natural and the other of spiritual. The natural citizenship comes from the place where we were born and is important because it gives rights of that country—but this natural citizenship is temporal.

The spiritual citizenship comes when we are born again into the family of God which provides us with certain kingdom privileges. This kingdom citizenship provided through our Lord Jesus Christ is eternal. The kingdom citizenship has higher authority in our lives because of the authority of God's word.

How does one get into the Kingdom of God? Recorded in John 3:3: *"Jesus answered and said to him (Nicodemus), 'Most assuredly, I say to you, unless one is born again (from above or new), he cannot see the kingdom of God.'"* Written in John 3:5 our Lord said, *"Most assuredly, I say to you, unless one is born of water and the Spirit, he cannot enter the kingdom of God."*

I Chronicles 29:10 -12:

"Blessed are You, Lord God of Israel, our Father, forever and ever. Yours, O Lord, is the greatness, the power and the glory, the victory, and the majesty; for all that is in heaven and in earth is Yours; Yours is the kingdom, O Lord, and You are exalted as head overall. Both riches and honor come from You, and You reign overall. In Your hand is power and might; in Your hand it is to make great and to give strength to all."

The New Compact Bible Dictionary reads as follow: The Kingdom of God is the realm in which God's reign is experienced. This realm is sometimes something present, sometimes future. In various verses, the Kingdom is a present realm where men may enjoy the blessings of God's rule.

The Kingdom is God's reign or rule. When we seek God's Kingdom and righteousness, we seek for God's rule in our lives (Matt. 6:33).

Romans 14:17: *"...for the kingdom of God is not eating and drinking, but righteousness and peace and joy in the Holy Spirit."* May we value the goodness of God through our Lord Jesus Christ and by the Holy Spirit. This righteousness that the Word of God declares is not our righteousness because according to Isaiah 64:6, *"But we are all like an unclean thing, and all our righteousnesses are like filthy rags..."* But the Bible promised us in 2 Corinthians 5:21, *"For He made Him who knew no sin to be sin for us, that we might become the righteousness of God in Him."* Regarding the peace of God, the

Bible stated in Romans 15:13, *"Now may the God of hope fill you with all joy and peace in believing, that you may abound in hope by the power of the Holy Spirit."*

Listed below are various characteristics of the kingdom of God:

Not easy for a rich man to enter the kingdom – Matthew 19:24: *"And again I say to you, it is easier for a camel to go through the eye of a needle than for a rich man to enter the kingdom of God."*

The kingdom of God is to be preached – Mark 1:14: *"Now after John was put in prison, Jesus came to Galilee, preaching the gospel of the kingdom of God."*

The kingdom of God is at hand – Mark 1:15: *"...and saying, 'The time is fulfilled, and the kingdom of God is at hand. Repent, and believe in the gospel.'"*

The kingdom of God is a mystery – Mark: 4:11: *"And He said to them (the disciples), 'To you it has been given to know the mystery of the kingdom of God; but to those who are outside, all things come in parables.'"*

The kingdom of God is like seed – Mark 4:26-27: *"And He said, 'The kingdom of God is as if a man should scatter seed on the ground, and should sleep by night and rise by day, and the seed should sprout and grow, he himself does not know how.'"*

The kingdom of God does not come with observation and is within us – Luke 17:20-21: *"Now when He was asked by the Pharisees when the kingdom of God would come, He answered them and said, 'The kingdom of God does not come with observation; nor will they say, 'See here!' or 'See there!' For indeed, the kingdom of God is within you.'"*

The kingdom of God is with power – I Corinthians 4:20: *"For the kingdom of God is not in word but in power."*

According to the Scripture in Matthew 6:33, we are to seek the kingdom of God first, *"But seek first the kingdom of God and His righteousness, and all these things shall be added to you."*

The Christian Standard Bible recorded Matthew 6:33 as, *"But seek first the kingdom of God and his righteousness, and all these things will be provided for you."*

God has told us through His Word to seek first the kingdom of God. According to the Strong's Concordance, the Greek Word for 'seek' is 'zeteo' meaning endeavor, enquire. God is asking us to have a fervent desire for the kingdom of God along with His righteousness. The Merriam-Webster Dictionary defined 'seek' as to try to reach or obtain. What comes to my mind is when David, the prophet, said to the Lord, "O God, You are my God; early will I seek You; my soul thirsts for You; my flesh longs for You in a dry and thirsty land where there is no water."[17]

Imagine yourself so parch with thirst and desiring for something to quench that craving. Nothing will satisfy that bone dryness except for a tall glass of ice-cold water; then after the drink, there is the refreshing.

Let our hearts thirst and crave for the longing of the kingdom of God and His righteousness that we may be able to receive that refreshing that can only come from the Lord.

The things written in the Word of God are for the necessities of life—by faith, may the promises of God be fulfilled in our lives.

---

[17] Psalm 63:1

HOLY BIBLE

In your own words, how would you describe the Kingdom of God?

The Will of God

Matthew 6:10(b):

"Your will be done."

How may we pray His will be done without knowing what is His will?

The will of God is the Word of God.

Saints, may we pray the beloved Scripture, Psalm 143:10: *"Teach me to do Your will, for You are my God; Your Spirit is good. Lead me in the land of uprightness."*

Our Father, who is in Heaven, has revealed His will to us through His Word, the Scriptures, which instructs us how to live before God through the Lord Jesus Christ by the Holy Spirit. Prayer may help us to impart God's way of life into our way of living.

Mark 3:35: *"For whoever does the will of God is My brother and My sister and mother."*

John 6:38-40: *"For I have come down from heaven, not to do mine own will, but the will of Him who has sent Me. This is the will of the Father who sent Me, that of all He has given Me I should lose nothing but raise it up at the last day. And this is the will of Him who sent Me, that everyone who sees the Son and believes in Him may have everlasting life; and I will raise him up at the last day."*

John 7:17: *"If anyone wills to do His will, he shall know concerning the doctrine, whether it is from God or whether I speak on My own authority."*

Romans 8:27: *"Now He who searches the hearts knows what the*

mind of the Spirit is, because He makes intercession for the saints according to the will of God."

Romans 12:2: *"And do not be conformed to this world, but be trans-
formed by the renewing of your mind, that you may prove what is
that good and acceptable and perfect will of God."*

Ephesians 5:17: *"Therefore do not be unwise but understand what
the will of the Lord is."*

Colossians 1: 9-10: *"For this reason we also, since the day we heard
it, do not cease to pray for you, and to ask that you may be filled
with the knowledge of His will in all wisdom and spiritual understanding; that you may walk worthy of the Lord, fully pleasing Him,
being fruitful in every good work and increasing in the knowledge
of God."*

I Thessalonians 4:3: *"For this is the will of God, your sanctification:
that you should abstain from sexual immorality."*

I Thessalonians 5:17: *"Rejoice always, pray without ceasing, in
everything give thanks; for this is the will of God in Christ Jesus
for you."*

Hebrews 10:36: *"For you have need of endurance, so that after you
have done the will of God, you may receive the promise."*

Hebrews 13:20-21: *"Now may the God of peace who brought up
our Lord Jesus from the dead, that great Shepherd of the sheep,
through the blood of the everlasting covenant, make you complete
in every good work to do His will, working in you what is well
pleasing in His sight through Jesus Christ, to whom be glory forever
and ever. Amen."*

I Peter 2:15: *"For this is the will of God, that by doing good you may put to silence the ignorance of foolish men"*

I Peter 3:17: *"For it is better, if it is the will of God, to suffer for doing good than for doing evil."*

I Peter 4:19: *"Therefore let those who suffer according to the will of God commit their souls to Him in doing good, as to a faithful Creator."*

I John 2:17: *"And the world is passing away, and the lust of it; but he who does the will of God abides forever."*

We can see in the Book of Genesis, in the Old Testament, where God commanded Adam not to eat of the tree of knowledge of good and evil. But Adam chose to listen to someone other than God, which consequently had him put out of the garden that was planted for him.

Genesis 2:16-17: *"And the Lord God commanded the man, saying 'Of every tree of the garden you may freely eat; but of the tree of the knowledge of good and evil "you shall not eat, for in the day that you eat of it you shall surely die.'"*

Genesis 3:23: *"Therefore the Lord God sent him out of the garden of Eden to till the ground from which he was taken."*

God has given us the knowledge of His will through the Word of God, but it is still our choice to obey the written Scriptures. He has given us the Holy Spirit to be our advocate throughout this life. (John 14:26).

Again, the will of God is the word of God.

What is the will of God for your life?

On Earth as it is in Heaven

Matthew 6:10(c):

"On Earth as it is in Heaven."

May our prayers be prayers from heaven which can cause a difference in the lives of people. If we really have a deep consciousness of one of the purposes of prayer, it is to have an impact on the lives of people turning them toward the living God. The direction that God is going, may we have a heart's desire to go in that same direction. John 14:6: *"Jesus said to him, 'I am the way, the truth, and the life...'"*

2 Peter 3:9: *"The Lord is not slack concerning His promise, as some count slackness, but is longsuffering toward us, not willing that any should perish but that all should come to repentance."*

Why prayers from Heaven? May we draw close to the Holy Spirit so that we may have an ear to hear the heart of God for our lives and the lives of others. Written in the New Testament in Romans 8:26-27, *"Likewise the Spirit also helps in our weaknesses. For we do not know what we should pray for as we ought, but the Spirit Himself makes intercession for us with groanings which cannot be uttered. Now He who searches the hearts knows what the mind of the Spirit is, because He makes intercession for the saints according to the will of God."*

There is a covenant with the earth: Genesis 9:13-15, *"I set My rainbow in the cloud, and it shall be for the sign of the covenant between Me and the earth. It shall be, when I bring a cloud over the earth, that the rainbow shall be seen in the cloud; and I will remember My covenant which is between Me and you and every living creature of all flesh; the waters shall never again become a flood to destroy all flesh."*

Oh, there is a connection between Heaven and Earth!

Deuteronomy 4:39: *"Therefore know this day, and consider it in your heart, that the Lord Himself is God in heaven above and on the earth beneath; there is no other."*

Psalm 89:11: *"The heavens are Yours, the earth also is Yours; the world and all its fulness, You have founded them."* Thank You, God, that You rule in the kingdom of men.[1]

Psalm 115:16: *"The heaven, even the heavens are the Lord's; but the earth He has given to the children of men."* Now what are we going to do with what the Father has given us? May we seek His face through prayer for the answer.

Psalm 124:8: *"Our help is in the name of the Lord, who made heaven and earth."* What situation may we have on this earth that our God cannot manage? Not a one.

Isaiah 45:18: *"For thus says the Lord, Who created the heavens, Who is God, Who formed the earth and made it, Who has established it, Who did not create it in vain, WHO formed it to be inhabited."*

Jeremiah 32:17: *"Ah, Lord God! Behold, You have made the heavens and the earth by Your great power and outstretched arm. There is nothing too hard for You."* When we get into difficulties within our lives may we remember that there is nothing too hard for our God—may we come into a place in our Christian walk that we will trust God with all our hearts and understanding.

Matthews 5:34: *"But I say to you, do not swear at all: neither by heaven, for it is God's throne; nor by the earth, for it is His footstool; nor by Jerusalem, for it is the city of the great King."*

Matthew 18:18-19: *"Assuredly, I say to you, whatever you bind on earth will be bound in heaven, and whatever you loose on earth will be loosed in heaven. Again, I say to you if two of you agree on earth concerning anything that they ask, 'it will be done for them by My Father in heaven.'"*

Ephesians 3:14-15: *"For this reason I bow my knees to the Father of our Lord Jesus Christ, from whom the whole family in heaven and earth is named."* Brothers and sisters, we are the family of God which connects Earth to Heaven.

Are your prayers connecting with Heaven?

Provision

Matthew 6:11:

"Give us this day our daily bread."

The Merriam-Webster Dictionary defined provision as the act or process of providing; also, a measure provided beforehand; a stock of needed supplies.

The Oxford Dictionary defined provision as the action or providing or supplying something for use.

The greatest provision ever:

John 6:35: *"And Jesus said to them, 'I am the bread of life. He who comes to Me shall never hunger, and he who believes in Me shall never thirst.'"* Also recorded in the Book of Matthew 4:4, *"Man shall not live by bread alone, but by every word that proceeds from the mouth of God."*

Our bodies need the sustenance of food and water. God is our provider of things of the natural as well as the spiritual. God our Father is our sustainer of life.

As we look to Him for the things of the natural world, look also to Him for the things of the spiritual realm. Heed to the promises of His word. Matthew 7:9-11: *"Or what man is there among you who, if his son asks for bread, will give him a stone? Or if he asks for a fish, will he give him a serpent? If you then, being evil, know how to give good gifts to your children, how much more will your Father who is in heaven give good things to those who ask Him!"*

Psalm 34:10: *"The young lions lack and suffer hunger; but those who seek the Lord shall not lack any good thing."*

Psalm 37:25: *"I have been young, and now am old; yet I have not seen the righteous forsaken, nor his descendants begging bread."*

Psalm 115:14-15: *"May the Lord give you increase more and more, You and your children. May you be blessed by the Lord, Who made heaven and earth."*

Matthew 6:26: *"Look at the birds of the air, for they neither sow nor reap nor gather into barns; yet your heavenly Father feeds them. Are you not of more value than they?"*

Matthew 6:31-34: *"Therefore do not worry, saying, 'What shall we eat?' or 'What shall we drink?' or 'What shall we wear?' For after all these things the Gentiles seek. For your heavenly Father knows that you need all these things. But seek first the kingdom of God and His righteousness, and all these things shall be added to you."*

John 14:13-14: *"And whatever you ask in My name, that I will do, that the Father may be glorified in the Son. If you ask anything in My name, I will do it."*

John 15:7: *"If you abide in Me, and My words abide in you, you will ask what you desire, and it shall be done for you."*

Ephesians 3:20: *"Now to Him who is able to do exceedingly abundantly above all that we ask or think, according to the power that works in us, to Him be glory in the church by Christ Jesus to all generations, forever and ever. Amen."*

Philippians 4:19-20: *"And my God shall supply all your need according to His riches in glory by Christ Jesus. Now to our God and Father be glory forever and ever. Amen."*

I John 5:14-15: *"Now this is the confidence that we have in Him, that if we ask anything according to His will, He hears us. And if we know that He hears us, whatever we ask, we know that we have the petitions that we have asked of Him."*

May we humble ourselves and seek the glorious face of our heavenly Father for every provision in our lives. As written in the Scripture, God will provide for all our need according to His riches in glory by Christ Jesus – Philippians 4:19.

List your needs that the Lord has provided for you.

Forgiveness

Matthew 6:12:

"And forgive us our debts, as we forgive our debtors."

The prayer is asking God to do to us as we do to others-we should want to treat people the way we want them to treat us. How is forgiveness made possible when our hearts have been damage to the point which seems unreconcilable? It is through the grace of God by realizing that greater is He in us than he that is in the world (I John 4:4).

Conquering unforgiveness is to triumph in Christ. How can one conqueror unforgiveness? It is through the attribute of constant prayer by asking God for His help.

According to the Strong's Concordance the Greek word for forgive is 'aphiemi' meaning to send forth. In other words, to release.

The Wycliff Dictionary expressed that forgiveness refers to the state or the act of pardon, remission of sin, or restoration of a friendly relationship.

The Zondervan Illustrated Bible Dictionary defined forgiveness as the act of pardoning or setting aside punishment and resentment for an offense.

As God has released us, may we release others from the hurt, pain, etc. that has been done to us. Is this an easy endeavor, no, but necessary in our walk with God, through the Lord Jesus and by the Holy Spirit.

The Merriam-Webster Dictionary defined forgiveness as to willing or able to forgive, allowing room for error or weakness. To forgive is to give up resentment of; to pardon, absolve; to grant relief from payment.

Forgiveness is a divine act given to us from God to be able to pardon others who have wronged us. Forgiveness is an attribute of love.

Unforgiveness is like placing oneself into a 6X8 encapsulated room, a place that stumps or hinders life. In this enclosed room is the stillness of the racing thoughts pounding against the mind with no end in sight. Thinking only of what has been.

The sadness about unforgiveness is that we believe that we have the right to hold our offender hostage because of the wrong that was committed to us. Yes, our hearts are delicate, as well as our feelings, which can be damaged by the trespass of another person. Not neglecting our injury or suffering but focusing and embracing the power of the Holy Spirit which can enable us to overcome the harm to embrace the life of Jesus living within us.

When we forgive, it is an advantage to us and to those we release? Can we be the children that only the Wise One has called us to be?

According to the Strong's Concordance, the word unforgiveness is not in the King James Bible—wonder why. The word forgive is in the Scripture a great deal of times throughout the Word of God. From this we can perceive that forgiveness should be in the forefront of our minds.

Look at the following instructions from the word of God regarding forgiveness.

Ephesian 4:32: *"And be kind to one another, tenderhearted, forgiving one another, even as God in Christ forgave you."* Ephesians 5:1: *"Therefore be imitators of God as dear children."*

Colossians 3:13: *"...bearing with one another, and forgiving one another, if anyone has a complaint against another; even as Christ forgave you, so you also must do."*

Why are we able to forgive when someone has offended us? *Because we are new creatures in Christ. Old things are passed away; behold all things are become new* (2 Cor. 5:17).

Good news from the Scriptures. I John 5:12: *"I write to you, little children, because your sins are forgiven you for His name's sake."*

One of our greatest witnesses of forgiveness was and is our Lord Jesus Christ who hung on the cross: Luke 23:34; *"Father, forgive them, for they do not know what they do."*

Having the heart of the Father, Stephan asked God to forgive his accusers. Acts 7:57-60:

"Then they cried out with a loud voice, stopped their ears, and ran at him with one accord; and they cast him out of the city and stoned him. And the witnesses laid down their clothes at the feet of a young man named Saul. And they stoned Stephen as he was calling on God and saying, 'Lord Jesus, receive my spirit.' Then he knelt down and cried out with a loud voice, 'Lord, do not charge them with this sin.' And when he had said this, he fell asleep."

Summed up in the voice of I Corinthians 4:12: *"...being reviled, we bless; being persecuted, we endure; being defamed, we entreat..."* Our command is forgiving others when they trespass against us. Yes, the ill treatment toward us is damaging to our hearts, but we are to remember that the grace of God is sufficient for us.[18]

Forgiveness is one of the attributes of the Kingdom of God—embrace it.

---

[18] 2 Corinthians 12:9

Who is the person(s) you must forgive? (Ask the Holy Spirit to search your heart.)

Temptation

Matthew 6:13a:

"And lead us not into temptation."

We must guard ourselves against temptation.

In the Strong's Concordance, the Hebrew word for temptation is 'maccah' which means a time of testing, trial. The Greek Word for temptation is 'peirasmos' meaning putting to proof, discipline, or provocation by implication adversity.

Holman Bible Dictionary defined temptation—used in KJV—as to refer to testing, trying, and enticing to evil. When the KJV was translated in 1611, "temptation" meant all of these, but the word has narrowed in meaning in modern times. Modern translations use "testing," "proving," "trying," and "tempting."

Merriam-Webster Dictionary defined temptation as the act of tempting; something that tempts. Tempt is to entice to do wrong by promise of pleasure or gain. To provoke; to risk the dangers of. To induce to do something.

The New Compact Bible Dictionary: On the one hand, temptation signifies any attempt to entice into evil; on the other hand, temptation indicated a testing which aims at spiritual good. Unless these two meanings are kept in view, the positive as over against the negative aspect, confusion inevitably results.

The Wycliffe Dictionary: May at times have the meaning "enticement to sin" which strongly colors our English words "temp" and "temptation". But their main and overriding meaning is that of "testing" the worth and character of men and sometimes of God.

Zondervan Bible defined temptation, testing as the idea of putting to the proof—from either a good or bad intention—which is found throughout the Bible.

There are various definitions of temptation, but when the temptation strikes our hearts and minds, we know and understand the danger that is set before us.

During our time of temptation or testing prayer is the key that will strengthen us that we may be able to bear the plight or to make a decision that will benefit our lives. Without prayer we are taking a chance to bring about an unthoughtful decision that may cause a hindrance.

It is interesting that the Lord Jesus told Peter that Satan wanted to sift him as wheat before the incident took place of denying Him three times before the rooster crowed. How could this be that the Lord prayed and warned Peter about the desire of Satan before the actual event took place? In other words, the Lord prayed about something before it happened. He saw the desire of Satan in the spiritual realm and prayed for Peter's faith not to fail. Peter was able to return to the Lord after denying Him three times. Also, gave him instructions what to do after his return. Look at Luke 22:31-32: *"And the Lord said, 'Simon, Simon! Indeed, Satan has asked for you, that he may sift you as wheat. But I have prayed for you, that your faith should not fail; and when you have returned to Me, strengthen your brethren.'"*

This is an example of how prayer can cause an interruption in temptation before the event takes place. Stay in close contact with God our Father through the Lord Jesus Christ by the Holy Spirit.

Prayer is the necessity for life—it can reveal those hidden events.

Often during these periods of tough times, prayer seems to be our last resort, when in fact it should be our first response. Cry out to our Father in Heaven that we may obtain help in a time of need. In fact, in Luke 22:40, *"The Lord said to pray that we may not enter temptation."*

Our Lord Jesus was led up by the Holy Spirit into the wilderness to be tempted by the devil. During this time of testing, the Lord had three encounters with Satan and each encounter was defuse by the Lord Jesus quoting the Written word (Matthew 4:1-11).

Romans 8:37: *"Yet in all these things we are more than conquerors through Him who loved us."* I Corinthians 15:57: *"But thanks be to God, who gives us the victory through our Lord Jesus Christ."*

During our time of struggle, may we run to the Rock that is higher than us. The Scriptures tell us in I Corinthians 10:13, *"No temptation has overtaken you except such as is common to man; but God is faithful, who will not allow you to be tempted beyond what you are able, but with the temptation will also make the way of escape, that you may be able to bear it."* The above Scripture is about the faithfulness of God. In the time of testing and trials lay hold to the fact that our God is faithful.

According to the Strong's Concordance, the Greek word for faithful is 'pistos' meaning trustworthy. The Oxford Language defined faithful as remaining loyal and steadfast.

Remember, to whom we belong. I John 4:4 let us know, *"You are of God, little children, and have overcome them, because He who is in you is greater than he who is in the world."*

What motivates the temptation to invade our lives? In the Book of James 1:13-15, it is clear about the origin of temptation. *"Let no one say when he is tempted, 'I am tempted by God'; for God cannot be tempted by evil, nor does He Himself tempt anyone. But each one is tempted when he is drawn away by his own desires and enticed. Then, when desires have conceived, it gives birth to sin; and sin, when it is full grown, brings forth death."* In these verses, James does not blame the devil, but it is our own sinful desires that birth death. Let us be perfectly clear that temptation does not come from God our Father.

Know this without a shadow of doubt as instructed by James 1:17: *"Every good gift and every perfect gift is from above, and comes down from the Father of lights, with whom there is not variation or shadow of turning."*

Remember when satanic forces try to capture our souls—grab hold on to the Word of God and exclaim with all our hearts: *"Greater is He that is in us than he that is in the world"* (I John 4:4) and think on the goodness of Jesus Christ and what He has accomplished for us on the cross and that our Lord Jesus is making intercession for us (Romans 8:34).

People of God, make it known by declaring to the enemy, and all our ungodly desires that they will not take us to an ungodly path of unrighteousness—not so.

In the Gospel of Luke, our Lord Jesus gave the disciples authority over Satan—Luke 10:19: *"Behold, I give you the authority to trample on serpents and scorpions, and over all the power of the enemy, and nothing shall by any means hurt you."*

What trial(s), temptations(s), or struggle(s) are you facing in your life?

Deliver us from the Evil One

Matthew 6:13b:

"But deliver us from the evil one."

We must be cognizant of the devises of the evil one—we must do as the Bible commanded us to do which is to watch and pray.

The Greek word for deliver is 'rhuomai' meaning rescue. Yes, Lord, "deliver us from the evil one."

The Webster Dictionary defined deliver as to set free; save.

Paul cried out in Romans 7:24, *"O wretched man that I am! Who will deliver me from this body of death? I thank God – through Jesus Christ our Lord!"* He asked the question who will deliver him, and he answered his own question. Jesus Christ is the one who delivered and delivers.

2 Corinthians 1:9-10: *"Yes, we had the sentence of death in ourselves, that we should not trust in ourselves but in God who raises the dead, who delivered us from so great a death, and does deliver us; in whom we trust that He will still deliver us...."* During our dilemma, we must trust God Who is able to keep us from falling (Jude 24).

2 Timothy 4:18: *"And the Lord will deliver me from every evil work and preserve me for His heavenly kingdom. To Him be glory forever and ever. Amen!"*

2 Peter 2:9: *"...then the Lord knows how to deliver the godly out of temptations and to reserve the unjust under punishment for the day of judgment..."*

The Word of God has instructed us to meditate on His word day and night. Meditation scripture: Romans 8:37: *"Yet in all these things we are more than conquerors through Him who loved us."*

Psalm 124:6-8: *"Blessed by the Lord, Who has not given us as prey to their teeth. Our soul has escaped as a bird from the snare of the fowlers; the snare is broken, and we have escaped. Our help is in the name of the Lord, Who made heaven and earth."*

May we remember as the Scripture has said in Galatians 5:1, *"Stand fast therefore in the liberty by which Christ has made us free, and do not be entangled again with a yoke of bondage."*

Hebrews 4:16: *"Let us therefore come boldly to the throne of grace, that we may obtain mercy and find grace to help in time of need."*

Are we allowing the Lord to deliver us from different situations? It would behoove us to concentrate on the love of Jesus Christ.

The Lord Jesus is our deliverer.

What have you been delivered from?

Kingdom, Power, Glory

Matthew 6:13c:

"For Yours is the kingdom and the power and the glory forever."

May we recognize the awesomeness of God our Father.

I would like to sum up this chapter with the following verses.

I Chronicles 16:23-27.

"Sing to the Lord, all the earth; Proclaim the good news of His salvation from day to day. Declare His glory among the nations, His wonders among all peoples. For the Lord is great and greatly to be praised; He is also to be feared above all gods. For all the gods of the peoples are idols, But the Lord made the heavens. Honor and majesty are before Him; strength and gladness are in His place."

And I Chronicles 16:29-34.

"Give to the Lord the glory and strength. Give to the Lord the glory due His name; bring an offering and come before Him. Oh, worship the Lord in the beauty of holiness! Tremble before Him, all the earth, the world also is firmly established, it shall not be moved. Let the heavens rejoice, and let the earth be glad; and let them among the nations 'The Lord reigns.' Let the sea roar, and all its fullness; let the field rejoice, and shall rejoice before the Lord, for He is coming to judge the earth. Oh, give thanks to the Lord, for He is good! For His mercy endure forever."

"For Yours is the kingdom and the power and the glory forever."

Glorify God in your own words.

Glorify God in your own words.

prayers

Repentance

Father, I come before You with my knees and heart bowed before You, humbling myself to Your perfect word. Realizing that I have need for Your forgiveness in my life. Asking You Father to have mercy upon me, according to Your loving kindness; according to the multitude of Your tender mercies, Father, blot out my transgressions. Wash me thoroughly from my iniquity and cleanse me from my sin.

For I acknowledge my transgressions and my sin is always before me. Against You, and You only have I sinned, and done this evil in Your sight. That You may be found just when You speak and be blameless when You judge.

Father, I am reminding You that I was brought forth in iniquity, and in sin did my mother conceive me. Behold, Lord God, You desire truth in the inward parts, and in the hidden part You will make me to know wisdom.

Purge me with hyssop, and I shall be clean; wash me, and shall be whiter than snow and make me hear joy and gladness, that the bones You have broken may rejoice. Hide Your face from my sins and blot out all my iniquities.

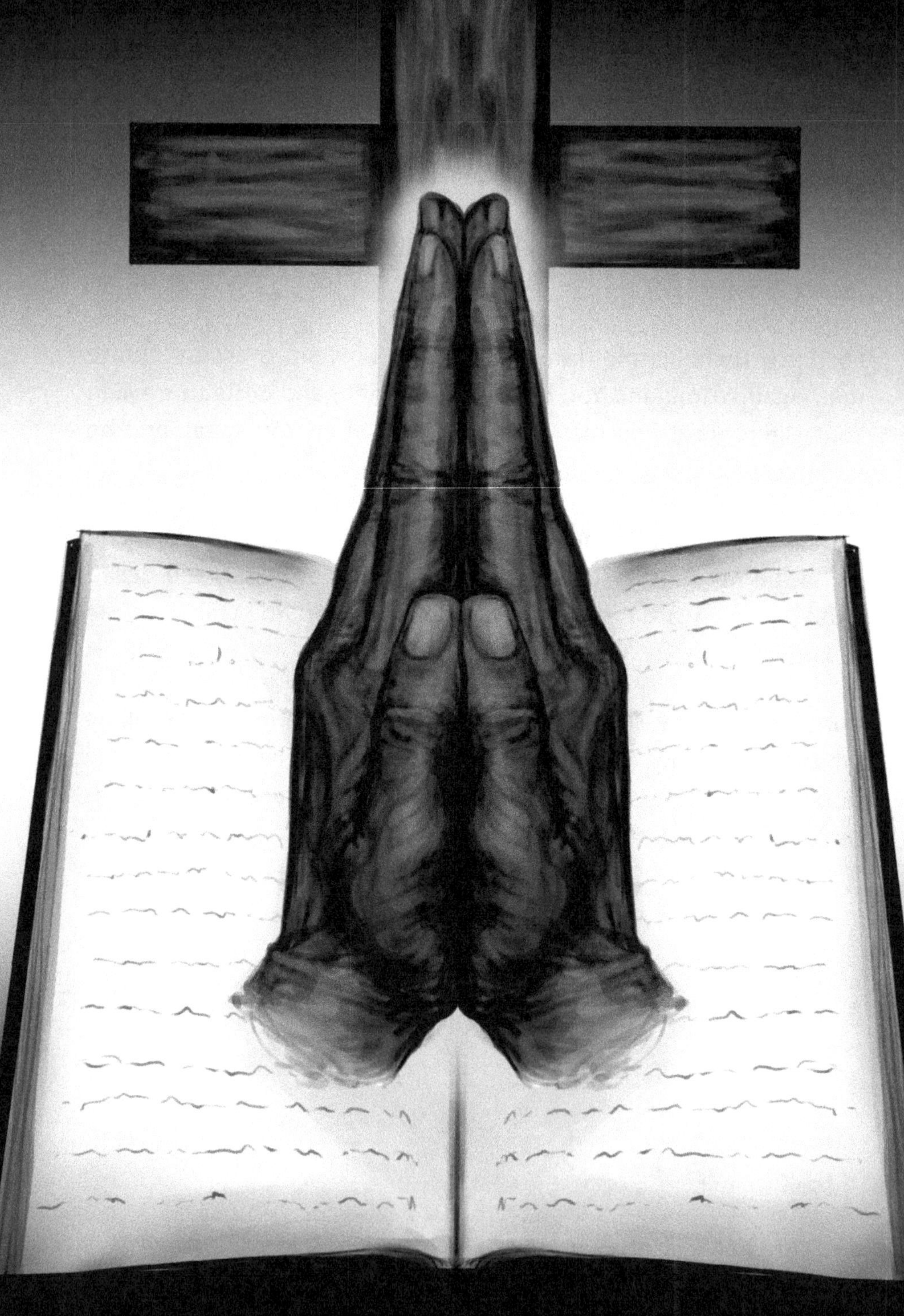

Father God, would You create in me a clean heart and renew a steadfast spirit within me? Do not cast me away from Your presence, and please do not take Your sweet Holy Spirit from me. Father, would You restore to me the joy of Your salvation, and uphold me by Your generous Spirit?

Then will I be able to teach transgressors Your ways and sinners shall be converted to You because You are the God of life.

My heart is heavy Father so deliver me from the guilt of my sins and transgressions for You are the God of my salvation. Because of Your cleansing power, my tongue shall sing aloud of Your righteousness and because of Your goodness the Holy Spirit will open my lips and my mouth to show forth Your praise.

My broken and contrite heart, God, You will not despise.

Do good in Your good pleasure to Zion; build the walls of Jerusalem, then You shall be pleased with my sacrifices of righteousness.

Thank You, Father, for forgiving me.

In Jesus' Name I pray.

Psalm 51

Unity in the Body

Father, I pray for the body of Christ that we as Your people may remain, unified. Behold how good and pleasant it is for brethren to dwell together in unity!

It is like the precious oil upon the head, running down on the beard, the beard of Aaron, running down on the edge of his garments.

It is like the dew of Hermon, descending upon the mountains of Zion; for there the Lord commanded the blessing—life forevermore.

I thank You, Lord, You are the God of our Lord Jesus Christ, the Father of glory, that You may give to us as Your body, the spirit of wisdom and revelation in the knowledge of Jesus Christ. May our eyes of understanding be enlightened that we may know what the hope of Your calling, what are the riches of the glory of Your inheritance in the saints, and what is the exceeding greatness of Your power toward us who believe.

Thank You that according to the working of Your mighty power which You worked in Christ when You raised Him from the dead and seated Him at Your right hand in the heavenly places, far above all principality, and power and might and dominion, and every name that is named, not only in the age but also in that which is to come.

Thank You, Father, that You have put all things under my Lord's feet, and gave Him to be head over all things to the church, which is His body, the fullness of Him who fill all in all.

My prayer is that the Holy Spirit would draw me closer to You, Lord.

Thank You, Lord

In Jesus Name I pray

Psalm 133:1-3; Ephesians 1:17-21

To Be Led by the Good Shepherd

How grateful I am to be led by the Shepherd of the sheep. My Lord Jesus, You have laid down Your life for me and because of Your goodness and Your shepherding, I shall not want.

Lord, You make me to lie down in beautiful green pastures; You lead me beside the still waters, You are the One who restores my soul and for that I am ever so grateful. You lead me in the paths of righteousness all for Your name's sake.

Yea, though I walk through the valley of the shadow of death, because of Your loving presence, I will fear no evil because You are with me. Your rod and staff they comfort me.

Lord, You have prepared a table before me in the very presence of my enemies. You have anointed my head with precious oil and my cup runs over.

Because of Your ever-loving presence, surely goodness and mercy shall follow me all the days of my life. And I will dwell in the house of the Lord forever.

In Jesus' Name I pray.

John 10:11; Psalm 23; Hebrews 13:5

Strength in God

Lord, You are faithful all the days of my life. Father, I do recognize You as my refuge and strength and a very present help in trouble and for that I am thankful.

Therefore I will not fear, even though it seems like in my life that the earth be removed, the mountains be carried into the midst of the sea, waters roar and are troubled, and though the mountains shake with it swelling, even still there is a river whose streams shall make glad the city of God, the holy place of the tabernacle of the Most High, God is in the midst of my life, I shall not be moved; God shall help me just at the break of dawn.

The nations raged, the kingdoms were moved; God uttered His voice, the Earth melted.

The Lord of Host is with me; the God of Jacob is my refuge. I love to meditate on Your goodness.[19] Come behold the works of my God who has made desolations in the Earth. You make wars to cease to the end of the Earth. You break the bow and cut the spear in two. You burn the chariot in the fire.

In my heart I know to be still, and know that You are God, You are to be exalted among the nations, You are exalted in the earth! The Lord of hosts is with me, the God of Jacob is my refuge. I am meditating on the goodness of the Lord.

Thank You, Father God, for You are my strength.

In Jesus's Name I pray.

---

[19] Psalm 46

Search Me O God

Father God, I will praise You, for I am fearfully and wonderfully made; marvelous are Your works and that my soul knows very well.

My frame was not hidden from You when I was made in secret, and skillfully wrought in the lowest part of the earth.

I am asking you to search me, O God, and know my heart; try me, and know my anxieties, and see if there is any wicked way in me and lead me in the way everlasting.

In Jesus' Name I pray.

Psalm 139:14-15; 23-24

My Help is from the Lord

In the day of my trouble, I will life up my eyes to the hills, I must ask myself, where does my help come from?

I know without a shadow of any doubt, my help comes from You Lord, who has made heaven and earth.

Father, thank You for not allowing my feet to be moved; You that keep me will not slumber. Behold You that keep Israel will neither slumber nor sleep.

Lord You are my keeper, You are my shade at my right hand because of Your protection, the sun shall not strike me by day, nor the moon by night.

The Lord shall preserve me from all evil, You shall preserve my soul, the Lord shall preserve my going out and my coming in and I am grateful for Your protection over my life.

In Jesus' Name I pray.

Psalm 121

Write your own personal prayer.

personal notes

My brothers and sisters, I pray that you may receive and embrace the love of god for your life.

My brothers and sisters, I pray that you may receive and embrace the love of god for your life.